COMMUNITY HELPERS

Firefighters

by Chris Bowman

BELLWETHER MEDIA • MINNEAPOLIS, MN

Note to Librarians, Teachers, and Parents:

Blastoff! Readers are carefully developed by literacy experts and combine standards-based content with developmentally appropriate text.

Level 1 provides the most support through repetition of high-frequency words, light text, predictable sentence patterns, and strong visual support.

Level 2 offers early readers a bit more challenge through varied simple sentences, increased text load, and less repetition of high-frequency words.

Level 3 advances early-fluent readers toward fluency through increased text and concept load, less reliance on visuals, longer sentences, and more literary language.

Level 4 builds reading stamina by providing more text per page, increased use of punctuation, greater variation in sentence patterns, and increasingly challenging vocabulary.

Level 5 encourages children to move from "learning to read" to "reading to learn" by providing even more text, varied writing styles, and less familiar topics.

Whichever book is right for your reader, Blastoff! Readers are the perfect books to build confidence and encourage a love of reading that will last a lifetime!

This edition first published in 2018 by Bellwether Media, Inc.

No part of this publication may be reproduced in whole or in part without written permission of the publisher. For information regarding permission, write to Bellwether Media, Inc., Attention: Permissions Department, 5357 Penn Avenue South, Minneapolis, MN 55419.

Library of Congress Cataloging-in-Publication Data

Names: Bowman, Chris, 1990- author.
Title: Firefighters / by Chris Bowman.
Description: Minneapolis, MN : Bellwether Media, Inc., [2018] | Series: Blastoff! Readers: Community Helpers |
    Audience: Age: 5-8. | Audience: K to Grade 3. | Includes bibliographical references and index.
Identifiers: LCCN 2017035033 (print) | LCCN 2017047024 (ebook) | ISBN 9781626177468 (hardcover :
    alk. paper) | ISBN 9781681034478 (ebook) | ISBN 9781618913074 (pbk. : alk. paper)
Subjects: LCSH: Fire fighters–Juvenile literature. | Fire extinction–Juvenile literature.
Classification: LCC HD8039.F5 (ebook) | LCC HD8039.F5 B693 2018 (print) | DDC 363.37–dc23
LC record available at https://lccn.loc.gov/2017035033

Editor: Nathan Sommer   Designer: Brittany McIntosh

Printed in the United States of America, North Mankato, MN.

Table of Contents

On Fire!

Smoke rises into the air. There is a house fire! Firefighters race to put it out.

The firefighters quickly spray water on the **flames**. The house is saved!

flames

What Are Firefighters?

Firefighters answer to all **emergencies**. They **rescue** people and put out fires.

Firefighters work in big cities and small towns. Some keep parks and **wilderness** areas safe.

What Do Firefighters Do?

Firefighters arrive first to emergencies. They help people who are **injured** or sick.

Firefighters get everyone out of burning buildings. They use many tools to stop fires.

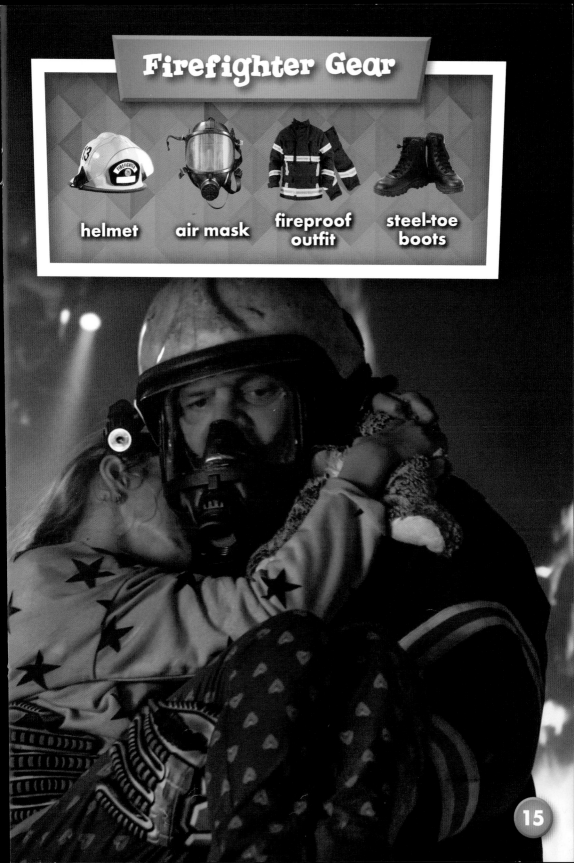

Firefighter Gear

helmet

air mask

fireproof outfit

steel-toe boots

Firefighters also teach people about fire safety. This helps stop fires before they start.

What Makes a Good Firefighter?

Firefighters are **alert**. They work for many hours at a time.

Firefighter Skills

- ✓ caring
- ✓ alert
- ✓ strong
- ✓ brave

Firefighters are
also strong.
They stay fit
to help keep
people safe!

Glossary

alert

quick to notice danger

injured

hurt or unable to act because of harm to the body

emergencies

unexpected situations that call for quick attention

rescue

to save someone from danger

flames

the burning parts of fires that people can see

wilderness

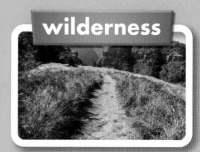

a wild area where few people live

To Learn More

AT THE LIBRARY

Bowman, Chris. *Fire Trucks*. Minneapolis, Minn.: Bellwether Media, Inc., 2017.

Murray, Julie. *Firefighters*. Minneapolis, Minn.: Abdo Kids, 2016.

Olsen, Alana. *Firefighters to the Rescue*. New York, N.Y.: PowerKids Press, 2017.

ON THE WEB

Learning more about firefighters is as easy as 1, 2, 3.

1. Go to www.factsurfer.com.

2. Enter "firefighters" into the search box.

3. Click the "Surf" button and you will see a list of related web sites.

With factsurfer.com, finding more information is just a click away.

Index

The images in this book are reproduced through the courtesy of: VAKSMAN VOLODYMYR, front cover; Jackan, pp. 2-3; ChiccoDodiFC, pp. 4-5, 6-7; kali9/ Getty Images, pp. 8-9; Frances A. Miller, pp. 10-11; Ventura, pp. 12-13; Gorodenkoff, pp. 14-15; tatajantra, p. 15 (air mask); Chad McDermott, p. 15 (helmet); aizaq abdullah, p. 15 (steel-toed boots); zorandimzr, p. 15 (fire-proof outfit); Justin Kase zsixz/ Alamy, pp. 16-17; TFoxFoto, pp. 18-19; ML Harris/ Getty Images, pp. 20-21; Claudio Rossol, p. 22 (top left); sirtravelalot, p. 22 (center left); fluke samed, p. 22 (bottom left); Monkey Business Images, p. 22 (top right); egd, p. 22 (center right); ChrisVanLennepPhoto, p. 22 (bottom right).